Handmade
Quilled
Greetings Cards

Diane Crane

SEARCH PRESS

First published in Great Britain 2005

Search Press Limited
Wellwood, North Farm Road,
Tunbridge Wells, Kent TN2 3DR

Text copyright © Diane Crane 2005

Photographs by Roddy Paine Photographic Studios

Photographs and design copyright © Search Press Ltd. 2005

ISBN 1 84448 006 2

The Publishers and author can accept no responsibility for any
consequences arising from the information, advice or
instructions given in this publication.

Suppliers
If you have difficulty in obtaining any of the materials and
equipment mentioned in this book, then please visit the
Search Press website for details of suppliers:
www.searchpress.com

Alternatively, you can write to the Publishers at the address
above, for a current list of stockists, including firms who
operate a mail-order service.

Publishers' note
All the step-by-step photographs in this book feature the
author, Diane Crane, demonstrating how to make quilled
greetings cards. No models have been used.

Cover

Rainbow Flowers

*The flowers have been glued across a circular aperture which
becomes more apparent when the card is open.*

Opposite

Strawberry Tea

*A wide range of quilling techniques have been used to conjure
up a summer afternoon.*

Manufactured by Classicscan Pte Ltd, Singapore

Printed in Malaysia by Times Offset (M) Sdn Bhd

Acknowledgements

I would like to convey my sincere
thanks to the following people, for gifts
many and varied. The fine folk at Search
Press for turning a long-held dream into a
reality, especially Felicity, my editor, and Roddy for
his expertise and gentle patience during
photography; Jennifer, who first introduced me to
quilling half a lifetime ago. Little did she know
what she had started! Yo, for her active
encouragement back in Barnes days – I have never
forgotten it; Lynn and Jan at Craft Expressions for
egging me on and for many good laughs along the
way; Linda at The Craft Barn for her support and
encouragement; 'my quilling ladies' past and
present – thank you all for your loyalty, friendship
and inspiration. How I wish I could bottle all that
quilled laughter – it is beyond price. Nicola, for
telling me about the rolled-up joy and for always,
always 'entering in'. Thank you, dearest friend.
Caroline, for believing in me, especially after I had
downshifted fairly spectacularly! Monica, for
faithful provision of cups of tea and hot dinners
stretching into infinity and for much else besides;
Pauline at Valence House Museum – 'Do you
know what? It's all made out of paper!' Special
thanks to Daphne, for that all important first-class
postage stamp!

Dedication

*This book is dedicated to the cherished
memory of my beloved parents, Marion and
Eric Crane. Thank you for the life we shared
while you were here, and the legacy of love you
left behind. Also to the dear memory of George
– thank you for all those black and white films
on countless Sunday afternoons, I'm
convinced they accelerated my quilling career.
And, yes, George, it has definitely been 'All go'!*

**'...whatever you do, do it all for the
glory of God...'**
**'...For in him we live and move and
have our being.'**

1 Corinthians 10 v.31, Acts 17 v.28

Contents

Introduction

For as long as I can remember I have been fascinated by paper of all kinds. One of my earliest memories is of sitting on the floor at home surrounded by bits of paper and being completely absorbed as I worked away with scissors and glue for hours on end. Well, not much has changed, except that I now favour sitting at the dining room table!

Over twenty years ago, a friend introduced me to the craft of paper quilling. I was instantly drawn to this unusual way of working with paper. Shortly afterwards, I discovered the existence of the Quilling Guild, which fired my enthusiasm still further. Having tackled many of the quilling patterns available at the time, I began to take my first tentative steps in designing my own patterns, and as I experimented with different techniques, I realised that the possibilities were endless, limited only by the imagination of the quiller.

After a few years of quilling for my own pleasure, I was given the opportunity to share my discoveries with others through teaching a weekly class. Card making using quilled motifs has proved to be the most popular application of the craft. I frequently hear stories from quillers who have sent cards that were treasured, and sometimes even framed, by the recipients.

Quilling may not be the speediest of crafts, but it is certainly one of the most rewarding. Narrow strips of coloured paper are brought to life by the simple act of rolling, and a colourful world of paper coils and spirals opens up before your eyes. Everything you need is readily available: paper, scissors, glue and a willing set of fingers... so you can quill away to your heart's content!

Diane Crane

There are endless possibilities with paper. Here are a selection of cards illustrating the different effects you can achieve by using the quilling techniques demonstrated on the following pages.

Materials

Paper strips

These are pre-cut in a number of different widths and come in a wide variety of colours, from delicate pastels through to vibrant shades in every colour of the rainbow. A standard quilling strip in Britain is 450mm (17¾in) in length, and the strips are usually packed in a figure of eight arrangement. I like to open out the papers and store them in shallow cardboard trays, as the strips are easier to work with if they are flat. The most common width of paper is 3mm (⅛in) which is suitable for beginners. Fringed flowers are usually made from 5mm (³⁄₁₆in) wide paper, although you can use 3mm (⅛in) paper for smaller flowers. Strips which are 2mm (³⁄₃₂in) wide will give a still finer appearance to your quilling. You can use paper which is just 1mm (¹⁄₃₂in) wide particularly for making fine spirals. Occasionally much wider strips are used such as 10mm (³⁄₈in) and 15mm (⅝in).

Paper quilling strips. From the top: 10mm (³⁄₈in), 5mm (³⁄₁₆in), 3mm (¹⁄₈in) and 2mm (³⁄₃₂in) strips. Not shown as actual size.

6

Quilling essentials

Quilling tool
Various tools are available commercially. The best tool to use is one which has a fine slit, and the slit should be deep enough to accommodate the width of your paper strip. If the slit is too wide, the paper slips about and you will find it difficult to make a start. The paper should fit snugly in the slit so that it stays in position once you start to roll. An added advantage is that a fine tool will produce a coil which has a small centre. This will always make your quilling look more attractive.

Glue and fine-tip applicator
PVA is the best glue to use and a fine-tip applicator will produce a very fine line with a gentle squeeze of the bottle.

Cocktail sticks
Use to apply tiny amounts of glue and also to pick up and position individual pieces of quilling.

Scissors
It is well worth investing in a good quality pair of scissors. I use embroidery scissors which have extremely sharp, short blades for precision work and another pair for general cutting.

Florist wire
Collect lengths in different gauges. You can make spirals by winding a strip around wire and then removing it.

Ceramic tile
A ceramic tile is a useful smooth surface to make eccentric coils on. Alternatively, you could use a jam jar lid.

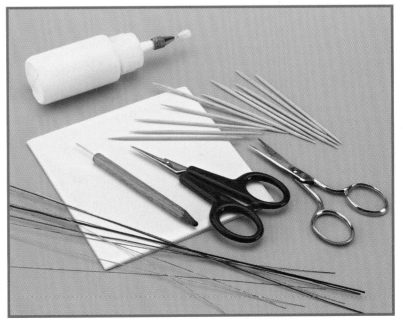

Other items

You will need a **ruler** when measuring and cutting your strips. You can make your own version from a piece of stiff card with the most common measurements marked on it, i.e: 75mm (3in), 150mm (6in).

Make a collection of **pearl-headed pins** with heads of different sizes. They are useful for moulding a solid coil into a dome.

A wide range of **blank cards** are available from good stationers and art shops. Aperture cards are useful, but you can cut your own shapes to fit a particular design with a little patience – and a steady hand! Mostly I buy flat sheets of card and cut my own. A **2H pencil** will give you an accurate line when measuring up a card and a **compass** is handy for drawing circular apertures.

When cutting with a **scalpel** take care because the blades are very sharp. Always cut against a **metal ruler** if you're making straight cuts. **Self-healing mats** are useful for cutting out apertures. The special surface prolongs the life of your blade and the 'wound' heals over as the name would suggest, so you can cut on it over and over again. They are sold in various sizes, but an A4 size is fine for most jobs.

Chalk pastels are wonderful for making subtle backgrounds for your quilling. They can turn a plain white card into something special. Pastels are available from art shops, and can be purchased individually or in boxed sets. You can use blunt scalpel blades for scraping small amounts of chalk pastel onto your card. Remember that pastels do not 'take' on card which has a smooth surface.

Tissue paper is available in a variety of colours. Squares of tissue paper can be wound diagonally around a piece of florist wire to make paper sticks. Tissue paper can also be used as a background for cards. For adding details such as facial features to your quilling, a **fine black pen** will be useful.

It is worth building up a collection of **paper and card offcuts**. You can use all kinds of bits and pieces when making quilled cards. Coloured envelopes from birthday cards are good for spiral roses and foil chocolate wrappers (with paper backing) are useful for spiralling. But beware – you soon might not be able to get into your house!

Storage is often a problem with quilling – there are so many tiny pieces to keep safe. I keep all kinds of small, shallow **boxes** to house my quilling.

Clockwise from bottom: blank aperture cards, different-coloured card, foil paper, different-coloured tissue paper, self-healing cutting mat, scalpel, 2H pencil, fine black pen, compass, handmade ruler, plastic ruler, metal ruler, pearl-headed pins, chalk pastels.

Tip

When not in use, store your fine-tip glue applicator upside down in a small container. This will help the glue to flow easily.

Basic techniques

Before you begin, take a close look at a quilling strip. One side is smooth with edges that turn down slightly and the other side is not. Take some time to feel the difference between your fingers. Always roll with the smooth side on the outside, as this will help to make your quilling more uniform.

When you are rolling a strip for the first time, resist the temptation to roll too tightly. People think that if they relax the tension, the coil will unravel but this is not the case. The rolled paper will only expand to its natural size. Quilling is a bit like knitting in the sense that the patterns may be the same but everyone's tension is different! Practise with 3mm (1/8in) strips before attempting to quill with finer strips of paper.

You will need

Eight 3mm (1/8in) paper strips, 150mm (6in) long

One 2mm (3/32in) paper strip, 150mm (6in) long

One 3mm (1/8in) paper strip, 450mm (17¾in) long

Quilling tool

Scissors

Fine-tip glue applicator

Cocktail sticks

Metric ruler

Tissue paper square, 50 x 50mm (2 x 2in)

Paper square, 20 x 20mm (¾ x ¾in)

Tile or jam jar lid

A basic coil

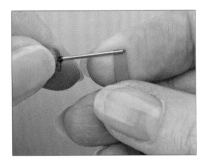

1. Line the strip up on the tool and start to turn.

2. Turn the tool so that the strip winds tightly around it.

3. When the whole strip is wound on, release it and remove the coil.

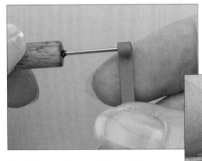

4. Put a dot of glue at the end of the strip. The less glue you use, the better your quilling will be!

5. Poke a cocktail stick into the coil and press against it as you close the coil.

A finished basic coil

Shapes

Each of the shapes that follow started off as a basic, glued coil. Hold the coil between your fingers and thumbs in the general shape before you make a definite pinch.

*Use your thumbs and forefingers to squeeze a coil into a **teardrop** shape.*

*Use both thumbs to make an **eye** shape.*

*Make another eye and then shape it into a **square**.*

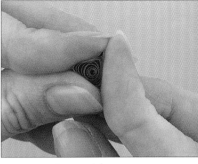

*Start with a teardrop and pinch it into a **triangle**.*

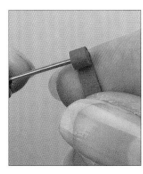

*Make another teardrop and shape it into a **long triangle**.*

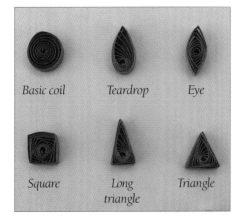

Basic coil Teardrop Eye

Square Long triangle Triangle

Tip

When making shapes, always pinch your coil at the glued join. This disguises the join and avoids it appearing in an awkward place.

Peg

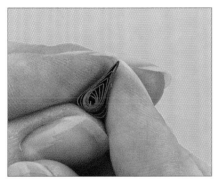

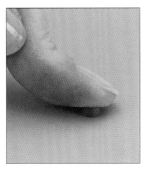

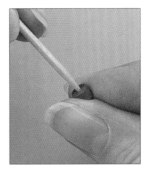

A finished peg

1. Roll a coil but do not let go when it is wound.

2. Glue the end of the strip down and then tap the peg down on the table.

3. Gently twist a cocktail stick in the hole to make the centre smooth.

Solid coil

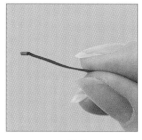

1. Start off the coil by hand. Make it as tight as possible.

2. Now roll the coil by hand. Do not let go when it is wound.

3. Glue down the end. Your coil should be solid in the centre as shown.

A finished solid coil

Eccentric coil

1. Make a coil on the tool using an entire 450mm (17¾ in) strip, release it and glue down the end.

2. Now rewind the centre as shown and then let go.

3. Use a cocktail stick to gently even up the loops.

Tip
Making eccentric coils takes a little practice. Do not be discouraged if your first attempt is not as perfect as the one pictured. Keep trying!

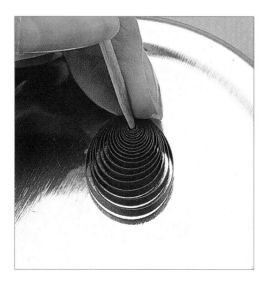

4. Put a dab of glue on a tile or jam jar lid and place the coil on top.

A finished eccentric coil

Spirals

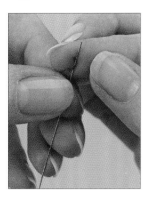

1. Cut a 2mm (³/₃₂in) strip down the centre to create two 1mm (¹/₃₂in) strips. Dampen the end of a 1mm (¹/₃₂in) strip with saliva and carefully wind it on to a piece of wire at a 45° angle.

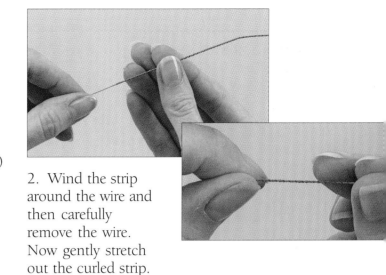

2. Wind the strip around the wire and then carefully remove the wire. Now gently stretch out the curled strip.

Spiral roses

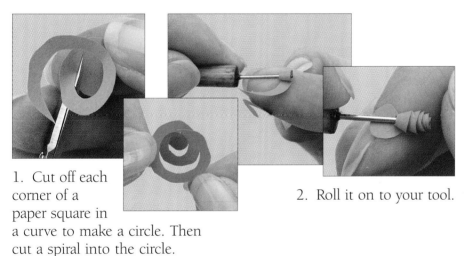

1. Cut off each corner of a paper square in a curve to make a circle. Then cut a spiral into the circle.

2. Roll it on to your tool.

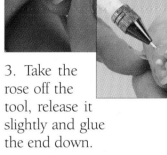

3. Take the rose off the tool, release it slightly and glue the end down.

Paper sticks

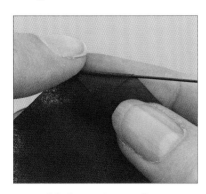

1. Fold the corner of a tissue paper square over a piece of wire and secure with glue.

2. Roll the tissue paper tightly around the wire.

3. Glue the end down and gently remove the wire.

Bloomin' Lovely

I like to experiment with all kinds of different subjects for designs but I always enjoy coming back to flowers. A simple flower in a pot is straightforward to put together and involves just a few of the basic shapes. I have chosen different shades of one colour but you can have some fun deciding on your own colour scheme. The following steps explain how to make one flower. Use the same technique to make four more flowers and complete the design.

Use the pattern above as a guide when you arrange your quilled shapes. The pattern is actual size.

You will need

For the flowers, 3mm (¹⁄₈in) strips:
40 strips in five shades of pink, 112mm (4½in) long, eight of each colour
10 green, 75mm (3in) long
5 green, 30mm (1³⁄₈in) long

For the flowerpots, 3mm (¹⁄₈in) strips:
15 brown, 112mm (4½in) long
5 brown, 45mm (1¾in) long

For the border, 2mm (³⁄₃₂in) strips:
2 brown, 450mm (17¾in) long

Quilling tool

Scissors

Fine-tip glue applicator

Cocktail sticks

Metric ruler and pencil

Blank card,
210 x 148mm (8¼ x 5¾in)

White paper,
160 x 45mm (6¼ x 1¾in)

Coloured chalk pastels

Scalpel

Facial tissue

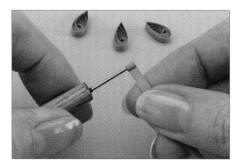

1. Make seven teardrops (as shown on page 11) from pink strips in one matching shade for the petals.

2. Make a peg (see page 11) from a strip in a contrasting shade of pink. Then make two eye shapes (see page 11) from 75mm (3in) lengths of green strip.

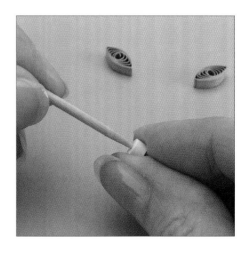

3. Make three triangles (see page 11) from 112mm (4½in) brown strips. Glue them together as above to make a flowerpot. Now glue a brown strip around the edge and snip off the excess.

4. With a pencil and ruler, divide the white paper into five sections. You now need to colour the sections in shades of pink from dark (left) to light (right) using chalk pastels. Use a scalpel to scrape shavings of chalk pastel over one section.

5. Use a facial tissue to rub the chalk pastel shavings into the card. Repeat on the four other sections.

6. Mark the 74mm (2⅞in) point on the shortest side of the blank card and fold it in half. Glue the chalked panel to the front of the card. Now begin assembling the first flower. Position the seven petals, and when you are happy with the arrangement, glue the petals down one at a time.

Tip
Your flower petals will look much better if the insides of the teardrops all face the same way.

7. Fold the 30mm (1³⁄₈in) green strip in half and glue the sides together to make the stem.

8. Spread a small amount of glue along the edge of the stem.

9. Place the top of the stem between the petals before lowering the whole stem on to the paper.

10. Glue down the flowerpot and both of the leaves. A cocktail stick is useful for positioning small pieces like the leaves.

11. Finally, glue the peg to the centre of the flower. Repeat steps 1 to 3 and 6 to 11 four times to complete the card.

12. Now add the border. Apply glue to the card following the pencil line. This will be neater than trying to apply glue to the strip.

13. Place the brown 2mm (³⁄₃₂in) strip over the glue, taking care to line it up with the bottom of the chalked panel. Trim off the excess strip, cutting it flush to the top of the panel. Glue all six vertical parts of the border in this way. Then attach a strip along the length of the panel at the top and one along the bottom.

A row of flowers creates impact, especially when it is given a bold border. Quilling strips are very useful for making a quick, accurate border. Using 2mm ($^3/_{32}$in) strips rather than 3mm ($^1/_8$in) will give you a more delicate result.

Your quilling does not have to be completely glued to a background. Here I have made a concertinaed card with flowers that stand proud. Instead of a double thickness strip, I have used a paper stick for the stem to make the flowers more robust. I have also outlined the petals by wrapping a contrasting strip around each teardrop before gluing them all together.

You can adapt this basic design in a variety of ways. One advantage of quilling is that you can take a design and by just halving or doubling the measurements, make a smaller or larger version. The tension will remain the same, it is the length of the strip that governs the size of your design. This window box is simply an extended flowerpot. Just increase the size of the triangles and keep adding more until you achieve the length you want.

Ready, Teddy, Go!

The shapes and swirls inside a coil intrigue me as much as the overall shape of the coil itself. In this project, I have used the eccentric coil method (see page 12) to make the body of the teddy. This technique is very useful when you are using a long strip of paper. If you left a large coil to its own devices, it would probably look rather untidy as the rolled layers of paper tend to gather at the edges of the coil, leaving an ugly space in the middle. By organising the layers into an eccentric coil, you can make it look much more attractive and it then becomes a design feature in itself.

You will need
For the teddy, brown 3mm (¹/₈in) strips:

Ears, 2 x 56mm (2¼in)

Head, 2 x 450mm (17¾in)

Body, 450mm (17¾in)

Arms, 2 x 150mm (6in)

Legs, 2 x 224mm (8⁷/₈in)

Snout, brown 2mm (³/₃₂in) strip, 112mm (4½in)

For the hat and wand:

Crown, 5mm (³/₁₆in) cream strip, 150mm (6in)

Brim, 2mm (³/₃₂in) cream strip, 150mm (6in)

Band, 2mm (³/₃₂in) black strip, 25mm (1in)

Black tissue paper, 25 x 25mm (1 x 1in)

Gold strip, 3mm (¹/₈in)

For the bow tie:

2 x black 2mm (³/₃₂in) strips, 56mm (2¼in)

Black paper square 2 x 2mm (³/₃₂in)

Quilling tool

Scissors

Fine-tip glue applicator

Cocktail sticks

Pearl-headed pin

Metric ruler and pencil

Blank card, 198 x 210mm (7¾ x 8¼in)

Fine black pen

Tile or jam jar lid

Yellow chalk pastel

Scalpel

Facial tissue

Use the pattern above as a guide when you arrange your quilled shapes. The pattern is actual size.

Tip
When you are using more than one strip to make a large peg, make sure that you begin rolling from the same end of each strip as you separate it from the pack. This will prevent the finished peg from having a stripy appearance.

20

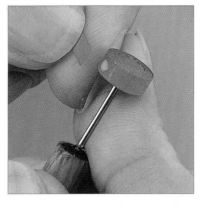

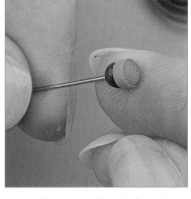

1. Start with the head. Roll a peg and glue it down. Glue on a fresh strip, roll it on and then secure with glue.

2. Roll two coils for the ears. Shape each coil into a crescent.

3. Make a solid coil for the snout and then push it on to a pin head to turn it into a dome. Now dab glue on the inside so that the snout keeps its shape. Allow to dry.

4. Make two coils for the legs. Shape each leg in two stages, as shown here.

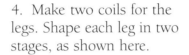

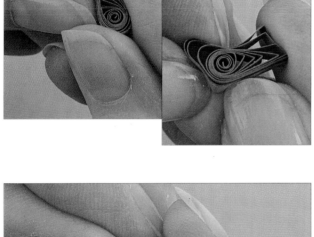

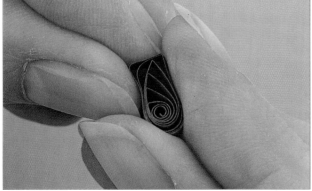

5. Make two more coils for the arms and shape them. Roll an eccentric coil for the body.

6. Mark the 99mm (3⅞in) point on the shortest side of the blank card and fold the card in half. Chalk three yellow circles on your card (see page 23). Then glue pieces of the teddy in place one by one.

 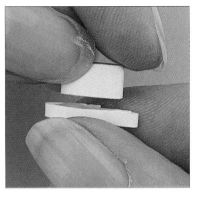 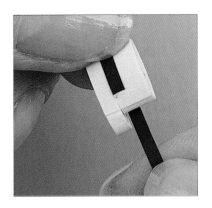

7. To make the crown of the hat, roll a 5mm (^{3}/$_{16}$in) cream strip into a coil and squeeze it flat.

8. Roll a looser coil from 2mm (^{3}/$_{32}$in) cream strip for the brim and flatten it. Glue the crown and brim together.

9. Wrap a 2mm (^{3}/$_{32}$in) black strip around the hat and glue it down. Trim off any excess black strip.

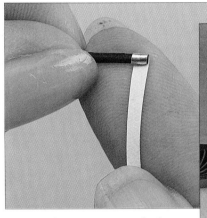  

10. Make a paper stick (see page 13) from the tissue paper square and snip the ends straight. Then wrap a tiny piece of gold strip around one end and glue.

11. For the bow tie, make two triangles, dab glue on the back of each of them and position as shown using a cocktail stick.

12. Glue a small black square to the middle of the bow tie.

13. Glue on your bear's hat and cane. Then draw on his face with a fine black pen. Repeat steps 1 to 13 to make two more bears. Assemble them on the card and glue in place.

These energetic teddies look as though they have danced on to the card. By changing the position of the arms and legs you can create the illusion of movement. All of the bears have the same component parts as the one described in the steps, but you may need to alter the angle at the top of the arms and legs.

Teddies never seem to lose their popularity and card shops are happy hunting grounds for inspiration. Here, bears are busy catching butterflies, making daisy chains, and flying high above the clouds. The basic figure is the same on all the cards and I have used the chalk pastel technique to create all the backgrounds.

I have reduced the dimensions of the top and centre bears to make them look as though they are drifting up, up and away into the distance. To create the cloud effect, I used a piece of shaped card as a stencil.

Rambling Rose

Making sticks from squares of tissue paper brings another dimension to quilled designs. These sticks are surprisingly sturdy considering that they are made from tissue paper and they provide a bold framework for more dainty forms of quilling. This project really stands out from the background.

The trick to making even paper sticks is to start rolling as tightly and centrally as you can – once you have reached the widest point, you are home and dry! If you notice that your stick is becoming thicker at one end than the other, simply roll back the paper and try again.

You will need

For the trellis:
12 dark brown tissue paper squares, 50 x 50mm (2 x 2in)
4 dark brown tissue paper squares, 40 x 40mm (1½ x 1½in)
20 dark brown tissue paper squares, 25 x 25mm (1 x 1in)

For the gate and gatepost:
13 beige tissue paper squares, 30 x 30mm (1¼ x 1¼in)
4 beige tissue paper squares, 35 x 35mm (1³⁄₈ x 1³⁄₈in)
4 dark brown tissue paper squares, 50 x 50mm (2 x 2in)
2 dark brown 2mm (³⁄₃₂in) strips, 112mm (4¼in)
2 beige 2mm (³⁄₃₂in) strips, 25mm (1in)

For the rose vine:
17 pale pink paper squares, 12 x 12mm (½ x ½in)
13 dark pink paper squares, 12 x 12mm (½ x ½in)
4 green 2mm (³⁄₃₂in) strips, 450mm (17¾in)

Quilling tool
Scissors
Fine-tip glue applicator
Cocktail sticks
Florist wire
Metric ruler
Blank card, 288 x 144mm (11½ x 5½in)

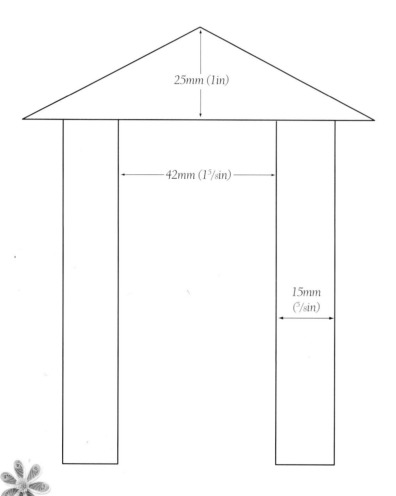

25mm (1in)

42mm (1⁵⁄₈in)

15mm (³⁄₈in)

Tip
When ruling your tissue squares, make a faint pencil mark or cut just inside the line to prevent pencil marks from spoiling the completed stick.

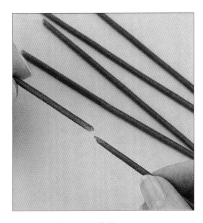

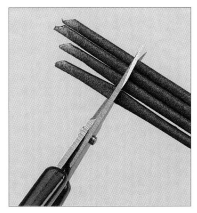

1. Make paper sticks (see page 13) from all the tissue paper squares listed under 'trellis' in 'You will need'. This will give you twelve 70mm (2¾in) sticks, four 55mm (2¼in) sticks and twenty 35mm (1⅜in) sticks.

2. Push ten of the 70mm (2¾in) sticks together in pairs to make five 120mm (4¾in) sticks.

3. Trim four of the 120mm (4¾in) sticks to 90mm (3½in). Then trim the remaining long stick to 95mm (3¾in).

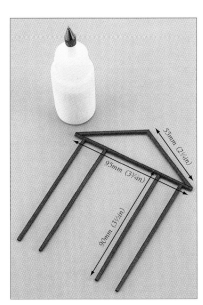

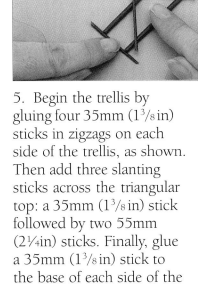

4. Glue the five trimmed sticks together to make the basic frame. Trim the last two 70mm (2¾in) sticks to 55mm (2¼in) and use them make the triangular top.

5. Begin the trellis by gluing four 35mm (1⅜in) sticks in zigzags on each side of the trellis, as shown. Then add three slanting sticks across the triangular top: a 35mm (1⅜in) stick followed by two 55mm (2¼in) sticks. Finally, glue a 35mm (1⅜in) stick to the base of each side of the trellis frame.

6. Turn the frame over and position more sticks on the back so that they cross those on the front, as shown. Then trim off all the jagged ends.

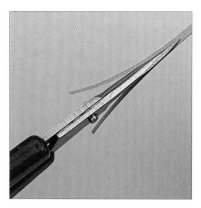

7. Carefully cut down the length of two green 2mm (³/₃₂in) strips to create four 1mm (¹/₃₂in) strips. Discard one of the strips.

8. Make three spirals (see page 13) around wire with your 1mm (¹/₃₂in) strips.

9. Glue the beginning of a spiral to the bottom of the trellis and then weave it in and out of the lattice work. Secure the end with glue. Repeat the same technique with the other two spirals to extend the vine, going along the top and then down the right-hand side of the trellis.

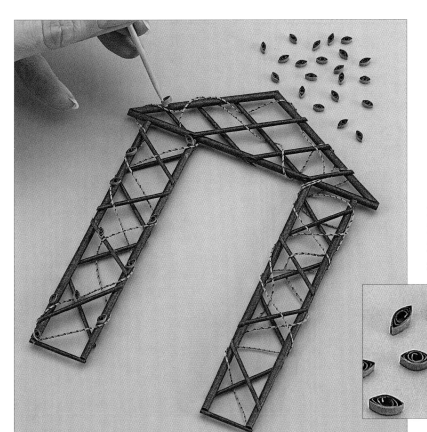

10. Cut the remaining green 2mm strips into 32 lengths of 28mm (1¹/₈in). Then make 32 eye shapes (see page 11) for leaves.

11. Cut circles from the pale and dark pink squares. Then cut spirals into each circle (see page 13) and make 30 spiral roses. Glue the roses randomly along the vine but try to keep the pale roses to the right-hand side of the trellis and the darker roses to the left.

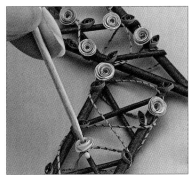

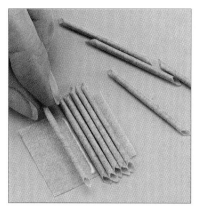

12. Make twelve sticks from the 30 x 30mm (1¼ x 1¼in) beige tissue paper squares. Glue ten sticks on to a 30 x 30mm (1¼ x 1¼in) square of tissue paper, leaving some space on each side.

13. Allow to dry, then trim off the jagged ends along the top and bottom of the backing square.

14. Make a paper stick from a dark brown square. Roll it around a cocktail stick and glue the end down. Then roll an identical square on top, to double the thickness, before removing the cocktail stick. Make another double-thickness stick with the remaining dark brown tissue-paper squares.

15. Repeat step 14 with the four 35 x 35mm (1⅜ x 1⅜in) beige squares. Glue a beige stick to each side of the gate and trim the ends straight. Now add the dark brown gateposts. Glue the remaining two beige sticks across the gate. Then glue 25mm (1in) lengths of beige 2mm (³⁄₃₂in) strip along the top and bottom of the gate.

16. Glue the trellis to the card, then the gate. Make two pegs (see page 11) and glue one to the top of each of the gateposts.

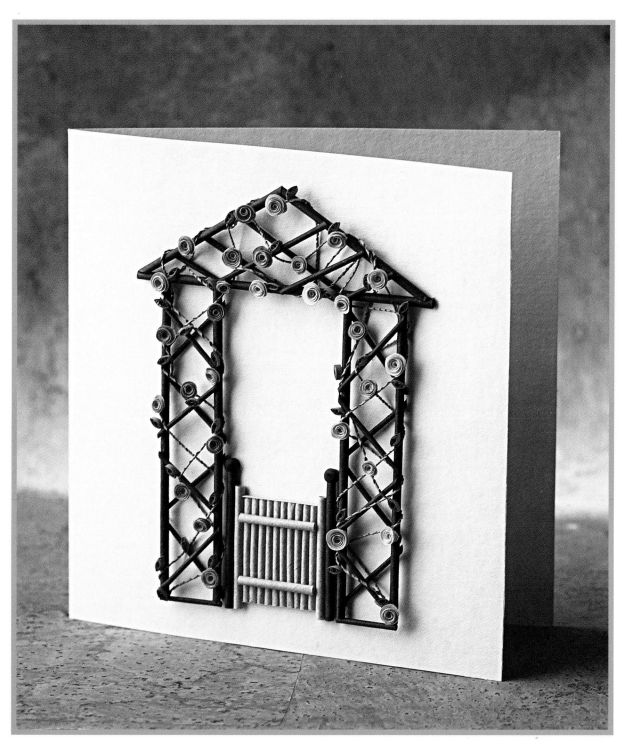

This design would make a lovely 'new home' card or perhaps a 'welcome home' card for a friend who has been away. You could personalise it by adding a house number to the front of the gate.

Left

Trellis work can be used as a frame for other quilling – here a rose bush is enclosed by a trellis border. Make the frame first, then weave the rose vine in and out.

Top right

I have extended the garden gate idea to create a picket fence covered with roses. Tiny loose coils represent the soil and give some weight to the design.

Bottom right

You can use flat strips of quilling paper to make a trellis quickly – glue several criss-crossing strips together and allow to dry before assembling the rest of the card.

Hey Presto!

This design will give you lots of practice in making squares from coils. The coils may seem quite big when you roll them but do not panic – you need the extra room to form the corners. Do not be afraid to apply pressure on the corners (not the sides) as a firm pinch will give you a sharper looking square. The other feature of this design is the fringed flower for the rabbit's head. Fringing gives another dimension to quilling, adding interest and texture.

Tip

When edging a shape, always put the glue round the shape, rather than on the paper strip – you are less likely to get glue in the wrong place.

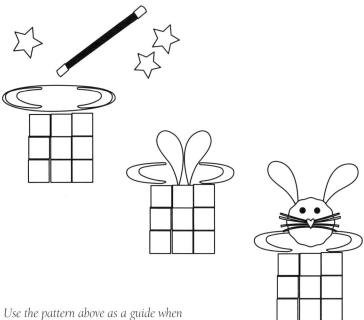

Use the pattern above as a guide when you arrange your quilled shapes. Not all of the stars are shown here. Place your stars randomly or copy the finished card. The pattern is actual size.

You will need

Per top hat:
9 black 3mm (⅛in) strips, 112mm (4½in) for the crown

2 black 3mm (⅛in) strips, 150mm (6in) for the brim

Black 3mm (⅛in) strip, 80mm (3⅛in)

Per pair of ears:
2 pale pink 3mm (⅛in) strips, 75mm (3in)

2 white 3mm (⅛in) strips, 112mm (4½in)

Rabbit's face:
White 5mm (³⁄₁₆in) strip, 300mm (11¾in)

Black 2mm (³⁄₃₂in) strip, 15mm (⅝in) for the eyes

Pink 2mm (³⁄₃₂in) strip, 30mm (1¼in) for the nose

White 2mm (³⁄₃₂in) strip, 15mm (⅝in) for the whiskers

Wand:
Black tissue paper, 30 x 30mm (1¼ x 1¼in)

White 3mm (⅛in) strip as required

Stars:
White 2mm (³⁄₃₂in) strip as required

Red 2mm (³⁄₃₂in) as required

Background panels:
3 red paper rectangles, 35 x 50mm (1⅜ x 2in)

2 gold face 2mm (³⁄₃₂in) strips, 450mm (17¾in)

Quilling tool

Scissors

Fine-tip glue applicator

Cocktail sticks

Metric ruler

Blank card, 150 x 210mm (5⅞ x 8¼in)

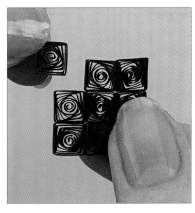

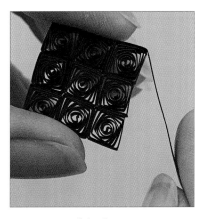

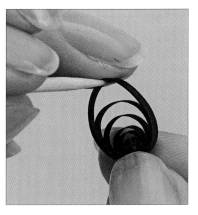

1. Make nine squares (see page 11) from the black 3mm (1/8in) strips. Glue the nine squares together in a block as shown.

2. Wrap a black 3mm (1/8in) strip around the edge of the block, gluing each side as you go. Repeat steps 1 and 2 to make two more identical blocks.

3. Now quill a coil from a black 3mm (1/8in) strip. Secure with glue, pressing the end down against a cocktail stick.

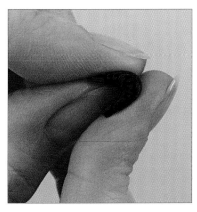

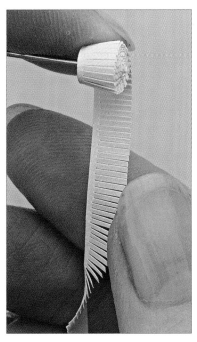

4. Shape the coil into a brim shape using a thumb and both forefingers. Repeat until you have six of these shapes altogether.

6. Push a cocktail stick gently into the middle of your fringed coil and then fluff out the fringing with a fingernail.

5. Make small parallel cuts along the length of the white 5mm (3/16in) strip. Take care not to snip right through the paper. Then roll up your fringed strip. Glue down the end and coat the base with glue. Allow to dry.

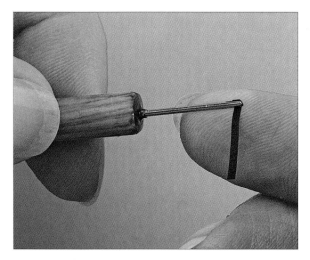

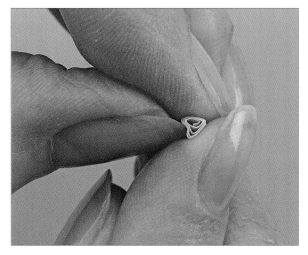

7. To make the rabbit's eyes, first cut the black 2mm ($^3/_{32}$in) strip into two 1mm ($^1/_{32}$in) strips (see page 28). Using a quilling tool, roll each 1mm ($^1/_{32}$in) strip into a peg and secure with glue.

8. For the nose, roll a tiny coil with a pink 2mm ($^3/_{32}$in) strip and glue down the end. Turn the coil into a nose shape with your forefingers and thumbnail as shown.

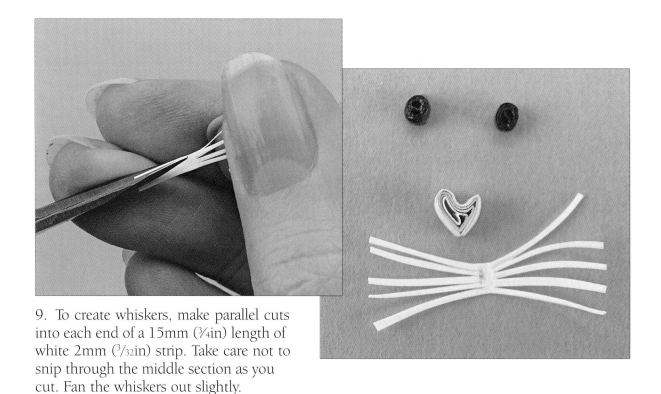

9. To create whiskers, make parallel cuts into each end of a 15mm ($^3/_4$in) length of white 2mm ($^3/_{32}$in) strip. Take care not to snip through the middle section as you cut. Fan the whiskers out slightly.

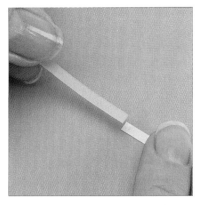

10. Glue the end of a pale pink 3mm (⅛in) strip to the end of a white 3mm (⅛in) strip, making sure that they are both smooth side up.

11. Roll your two-tone strip into a coil and secure the end with glue.

12. Now shape the two-tone coil into an ear shape as shown. The pink section of the strip becomes the centre of the rabbit's ear. Repeat steps 10 to 12 to make three more ears.

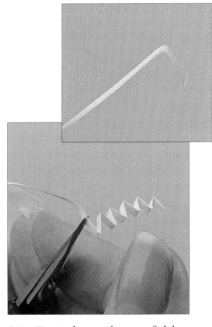

13. Mark the 105mm (4⅛in) point on your blank card and fold it in two. Then position and glue the three red paper rectangles on the front of the card. Glue the gold face trim around each rectangle. Following the pattern on page 34, now assemble the three top hats. Add ears to the second hat and ears plus a fringed face to the third hat. Use a cocktail stick to position the smaller pieces.

14. To make each star, fold over the tip of a 2mm (³⁄₃₂in) strip and then make ten concertinaed folds. Cut off the excess strip.

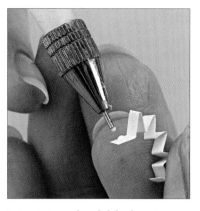

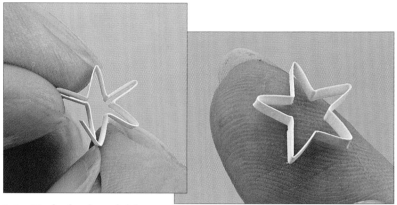

15. Bring the folded strip round into a ring and dab glue on the last fold.

16. Tuck the last fold inside the first and press the two together. Allow to dry and then adjust the star until the points are even. Using this technique, make seven white and five red stars.

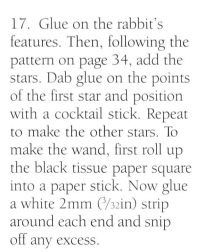

17. Glue on the rabbit's features. Then, following the pattern on page 34, add the stars. Dab glue on the points of the first star and position with a cocktail stick. Repeat to make the other stars. To make the wand, first roll up the black tissue paper square into a paper stick. Now glue a white 2mm ($^3/_{32}$in) strip around each end and snip off any excess.

Often, quilled designs favour the feminine side of life but this magical card would be suitable for a male recipient. It has bold colours and there is not a flower in sight! I like quilling to tell a story. It is not difficult to imagine what is happening here – 'Hey Presto' and the rabbit pops out of the hat!

You can add further interest to a card by using an aperture, so that some of the design is seen through the 'window' on the front. I used a compass to make a circle on the front, then carefully cut it out with a pair of scissors. The circular frame is created from a series of quilled triangles – you need to plan these carefully! I then edged the circle with thin gold spiralling made from a chocolate wrapper.

Above left

Here the rabbit has been joined by some playing cards. Some of the cards have been raised up from the background by simply adding pegs to the back before gluing them to the card.

Above right

I used a compass to make a faint pencil mark on the card as a guide when adding a red circle with chalk pastels. The magical elements are the same as those used in 'Hey Presto!' but I halved the original measurements for this design.

Sunflower Girl

This design uses solid coils made from paper strips in a range of different widths. The method is exactly the same for all the coils, it is just that the paper width varies from 2mm (³/₃₂in) to 15mm (⅝in).

It is worth practising this skill – there is a good quilling tradition whereby you drop the coil several times before achieving ultimate success! Once you have mastered the basic figure, it is fun creating different characters.

A solid coil is really useful for making a face as you do not want a hole in the centre! When it comes to making the arms and legs, I find it easier to start them off by rolling the strips round a long pin. Remove the pin, unroll the paper, then continue rolling with your fingers.

Use the pattern above as a guide when you arrange your quilled shapes. The pattern is actual size.

Tip
Wash your hands before rolling the solid coil to ensure that your sunflower girl does not get a dirty face! Try to handle faces as little as possible as the grease from your hand will easily show on a light-coloured paper.

You will need
Face:
2 pale pink 2mm (³/₃₂in) strips, 450mm (17¾in) and 224mm (8⅞in) long
Dark brown 5mm (³/₁₆in) strip, 70mm (2¾in) long
Light brown 1mm (¹/₃₂in) strip, 30mm (1¼in) long
18 yellow 2mm (³/₃₂in) strips, 56mm (2¼in) long

Arms and legs:
2 pale pink 10mm (⅜in) strips, 45mm (1¾in) long
2 pale pink 15mm (⅝in) strips, 50mm (2in) long

Hands:
2 pale pink 2mm (³/₃₂in) strips, 56mm (2¼in) long

Feet:
2 dark green 2mm (³/₃₂in) strips, 56mm (2¼in) long

Body:
2 pale green 2mm (³/₃₂in) strips, 450mm (17¾in) long
Pale green tissue paper
Dark green 1mm (¹/₁₆in) strip, 30mm (1¼in) long
2 dark green 2mm (³/₃₂in) strips, 56mm (2¼in) long

Quilling tool
Fine black pen
Scissors
Fine-tip glue applicator
Cocktail sticks
Long pin
Florist wire
Ruler
Blank card, 174 x 114mm (7 x 4½in)

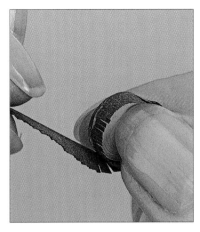

1. To make the face, first roll the 450mm (17¾in) pink strip into a solid coil. Join on the 224mm (8⅞in) strip and continue rolling. Gluing the strips end to end in this way avoids creating a ridge. Now cut a fringe into the dark brown strip and glue it around your solid coil.

2. Fan out the fringing, then make 18 yellow eye shapes. Glue them all the way around the back of the fringing as shown. Allow plenty of time for the glue to dry.

3. Make a spiral from the light brown strip and glue it, a little at a time, around the face to create hair. Then use a fine black pen to draw on her eyes and mouth.

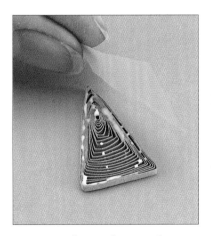

4. For the sunflower girl's body, first join together two pale green 2mm (³/₃₂in) strips and then roll the long strip into a coil. Shape the coil into a teardrop.

5. Now shape the teardrop into a triangle. Apply glue to the back and place the pale green tissue paper over it. Once the glue is dry, trim away any excess tissue paper.

6. To make an arm, roll the 10mm (³/₈in) pink strip around a pin, then remove the pin and re-roll by hand. Repeat to make another arm.

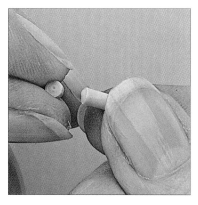 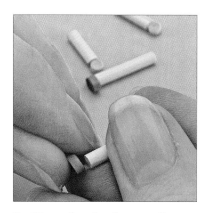 

7. Roll a peg from pale pink 2mm (³/₃₂in) strip for each of her hands.

8. To make the legs, roll each of the 15mm (⁵/₈in) pink strips into pegs. Make two coils from dark green 2mm (³/₃₂in) strip for the feet and squash them flat. Glue the feet to the legs and leave until completely dry.

9. Glue the arms and legs, one at a time, to the back of the body, making sure that the seam of the join on each arm and leg is not visible at the front.

10. Make two small eye shapes using a dark green 2mm (³/₃₂in) strip for each leaf. Now make a spiral from dark green 1mm (¹/₃₂in) strip for the stem. Glue the spiral down the centre of the body and trim off any excess. Next glue on the head and finally, attach each of the leaves. Use a cocktail stick to position the leaves. Allow your sunflower girl to dry before gluing her to the card.

This whimsical flower girl is perfect for wishing someone 'Happy Birthday' or 'Get Well Soon'. Try using other flesh tones for the arms, hands, legs and face. You do not necessarily need to use wide quilling strips for the arms; other kinds of paper will do as long as the paper is thin enough to roll and roughly the same shade as the strips you are using. Envelopes are often good for this purpose.

Left top

Little girls can be dressed in a variety of ways. You can move the hem line up on a dress by making a shorter triangle. Add more quilling at the hem, to create different styles.

Left bottom

Each ballet dancer has a short, square body and a series of teardrops to make a tutu. Note how the arms and legs are the same basic pattern, they are just glued at different angles. Keep practising, girls...

Above
These little figures lend themselves to free-standing cards. Here I have experimented with different kinds of flower girls. You could write a message on the rectangles beneath.

Index

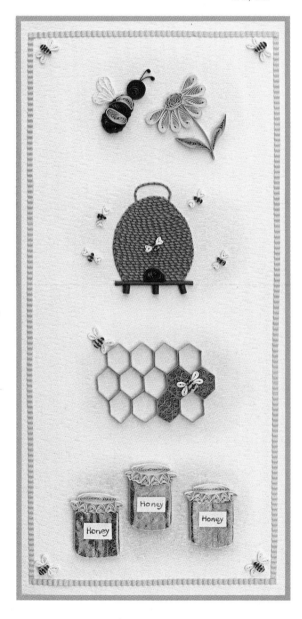